A Model Year

A Model Year

Coconut Books
20

poems by
Gina Myers

Atlanta, GA
09

Copyright © 2009 by Gina Myers

Published by Coconut Books

www.coconutpoetry.org

All rights reserved

ISBN: 978-0-578-02739-5

Cover Design: Paolo Pedini
Book Design: Justin Sirois

Contents

I. Young Professionals in the Rain

Fable	9
Brooklyn	10
Brazen Youth	11
Tuesday	12
Each Spring	13
Elegy	14
Young Professionals in the Rain	15
9.25.04	16
Winter Window	17
After David Shapiro	18
Midwinter	19
House	20
Apartment 11	21
Lullaby	23
A Partial List of Fears	24

II. Notes & Letters

Yours Truly	27
Love Poem to Someone I Do Not Love	28
Dear M –	29
I'm not even trying	30
The Answer	31
Travel Notes	32
Saginaw	37
4.14.06	38
A Partial List of Fears	39

III. Homecoming

Forecast	43
The Waiting	44
Prayer	45
Drought	46
Return	47
January	48
The Dare	49
March	50
Self-Portrait as a Mirror	51
Sonnet Beginning with Lines by Robert Creeley	52
The Functioning	53
The Dance	54
Rilke	55
Perpetual Motion	56
The Trap	57
Homecoming	58
A Partial List of Fears	59

IV. A Model Year

A Model Year	63

I.
Young Professionals in the Rain

Fable

Blame this day. Blame the stove
& the curtain. Blame the oily dishwater.
The prodigal has returned.
You've taken the sword, now
take the body too.
The word *surrender* caught
in my teeth. The filthy rusted nail.
Dearest sister, I'm only asking
what's been promised. The poison
has reached your lungs now breathe.

Brooklyn

Wires cross & re-cross:
one bruise covers another.
Pigeons & sky washed-
out grey. The weight
of a minute creases
the back of the neck.
The movement towards zero
tucked into the center.
Fog on the window
expecting a new day,
expecting warm breath
& the pressure of a fingertip
drawing a circle.
Or the movement away.
Repeating to repeat.
The arc of a hand—
gentle wave, slight turn.
Leaves twist in the wind,
brush across sidewalk.
Edges unfold, smudge out
with the brush of a thumb.

Brazen Youth

Four years advantage in the race
across the street. Half the pressure,
twice the speed. The hard-learned
lesson not every pigeon can
be trusted. Kicking through leaves
November crisp & sneaky sneaks
passing notes. Who wants to pay
for a soda anyway? Misused coffee
cups & the imagined lives of co-workers
a thousand times better than this
ten to six day in day out.
The imagined lives of forties on rooftops
& fingernails flecked with silver
spray paint. As if a photograph could catch
it all or catch anything at all.
Carrying the weight of our costumes
through this downward spiral circle pit.
The frenzied youth smashing
up against one another. Now: counter-
clockwise. Goodbye lovers & haters.
Goodbye New York.

Tuesday

Or today buying a wooden picture frame
& its refusal to hang flat against the wall.

This doesn't change anything. The doorframe
solid there, just waiting for someone to pass.

On the other side of the wall: children laughing.
Add this to my list of failures: I have never seen

the tide rise or held a fragile life in my hand.
Never a gentle knife, a knock in the wind.

My magazine rack securing my place in the world.
The shelves of books a sign of the real.

The cup of tea I pour solves nothing.
I make a list of all the things I'd like to break.

Each Spring

Looking for my name
in every pawn shop
I'm not fit
to be a politician's
wife Laughing along
Lake Shore Drive
Pointing to all the places
we'll never live
Our plans for Mexico
forgotten at the end
of a novel
4am post-bar text
message The camera's 3rd eye
wrapped inside a flag
Each spring
brings the promise
of a new baseball season
Outside Wrigley boys
stand along N. Waveland Avenue
with gloves on their hands
Too young to have yet learned
baseball is only
good for heartache

Elegy

Either the house was full or the tea leaves had dried.
Either a house, or if not a house, a sparrow.
If not words, then the meaning of words.
Either it is lost, it is lost, or it is not lost.
An open hand or a locked door.
If a locked door then never any rest.
Either a voice or voicelessness.
Beginning or ending or nothing.
If not good enough, then never.
No pockets for keeping.
No bed. No window.
Either a frame or a photograph.
Either a blank space or a letter in the mail.
Not a letter, but a postcard.
Not a postcard, but a gesture, an image of nature.

Young Professionals in the Rain

If time had chosen a different way.
If every mistake disappeared.
The radio tuned to storm & static.
Here is an elegy for the tide
that doesn't rise, for our months lost at sea,
a map of shipwrecks & desire,
the fold of an envelope, a paper cut.

Science now believes we each have
our own special place for keeping.
We each have our own word for loneliness.
No one saw what was stolen,
scars rising from skin.
No one can taste the poison in the water
but we know it's there. We know
no other way. In science there is nothing
to hold on to. The smooth rock
in my pocket, a body.

In motion or looking to rest.
No one saw the weather report
or pretended to know the rain won't stop.
The storm returns to memory.
The young professionals in the rain,
going to work in the latest watches,
waiting for something to love, something
to blow up in their faces. To believe in a kind of
perfection only a child can believe in.

9.25.04

what time   is it   another night   lost
tripping along   uneven pavement
slight hangover   this brick   inescapable
kids on hoods of cars   September & nothing
passing through   repeat this   breath
arc   of movement   hands in pockets
hands of clock   pointing
to your numbered   self   shattered
space   bodies folding over   night
washed out   treeline dissolved into sky
no stars, no rest   trying too hard & not
hard enough   your autumn   songs scratching
the surface   paint   burnt on retina
trying to make sense of   a study
of three faces   dimensions of spacetime
your night a different night   smoke in my lungs
trying to get   my papers in order   trying
to tell   gunshots & one
window over an alley   my indoor voice hushed
your turned self   turning away   turning
into   your furtive self
                      the horizon   bubbling
ready to burst

Winter Window

If anger fades as it rises, folds itself
        into a paper crane.
If happiness never wears a hat or meets
        itself in the street
a broken picture frame left on the curb.
If happiness were a hero smiling
        down from a parade.
The snow keeps falling. A door leads
        to another door to a room
I've never entered.
All the shops are locking their gates.
We hold our hands over our mouths
        for warmth, huddle over
what is not being said.
We have our secrets we prefer to keep.
We do not trust what is too good.
A shadow moves beneath the door.
Winter waits & listens & promises its worst.
And we go on preferring the intimacy
        of an empty bed the clock
that ticks but does not turn.

After David Shapiro

dear cloud, free from moral guilt
dear calendar, your pages worn
dear bridge, free from the heart's concerns
dear train, free from pain
dear passing, no need for a watch
dear address, words on your eyelids
dear lullaby, dear vase of flowers, dear candy store
dear sun, let go your winter coat
dear stove, free from yesterday's mistakes
dear fan blades, turn & turn
dear song, it's come out all wrong

Midwinter

Slush on every street corner. To find happiness
in a red scarf. The hope of oceans & sand folded
in a tiny crease. Fitting all I can in my hand.
Another night—broken window—New York skyline.
The train passes every fifteen minutes—the suggestion
of space that needs to be filled. The snow falling
outside is quiet. The boxes on the curb: quiet.
The boxes covered with snow. Tonight
the radio is a companion keeping the body warm.
The streetlight tall & empty. The lamp is quiet.
Searching for a new vocabulary, a way
to say exactly what you want to hear.
I'd like to give all the quiet things to you.
The hour: traumatized. You've finished one
chapter but refuse to start the next, prefer instead this
moment of waiting. To hold on to any one thing
just a little longer. To hold on to this pain.
The angry faces in line at the bodega. The cold
& angry faces waiting for someone to notice.

House

& opening & opening & the black spray paint on the door & the summer spent tiling the roof & don't walk away &   scrubbing blood off the bathroom floor & the splintered hand rail & oak trees & maples & the bird feeder nailed   outside the kitchen window & every morning & voices & turning & waking & the pictures crooked on the walls & the buzzing lights & noise from the street & saint of perpetual sorrow & tomorrow & spiders hiding in the cracks & this practice of memory & please listen & hardwood floors & bare feet & the quiet at night & the light in the hallway & the door bell at 3 a.m. & sirens & sleeping & where were you & every summer & growing out of clothes & vegetables for stew & hips & cups of tea & this absence of relief & not now & your quiet self & winter & why & stained carpet & the smell of piss in the hallway & crucifix over your bed & quilt & creaking stairs & echoes & starting over & rusted mailbox & saint of immediate relief & running & muddy shoes & candles & your hands & running & the cracks around your eyes & running & running &

Apartment 11

last night's sidewalk   inappropriate proposition   today
new
jeans & thunderstorms   desire   to be somewhere
              away
from rent   demands   & bills

the united states
postal service   losing
the evening clear & windy   no rain   only children
running   in the halls   music
from a passing   ice cream truck
my legs tired but I don't know why   slept late
no coffee
no afternoon   casual Saturday & Saturday night   holding
this place
together with scotch tape & stacks
of books   mint
tea   the weekend nearly over   not
wanting to face the
photocopier   & fax machine
In an attempt to define   freedom
I can only say no   no sir
this isn't it   all circuits are currently busy
avenues   gridlocked
the night won't   have
my stupid questions   won't carry on
this
stupid game   the cat   keeps
the cockroaches away
& the neighborhood   sighs
tenements
                 lean   on my shoulder
carrying this   alone   dear walls
please stop
your shaking
a layer of paint   won't

21

fix
                        ceiling falling in &
books   out of order
               I know   the money   in my pocket
                                                                       bill &
too
little sleep   & so it's hard   here & everywhere
so much depends   on the leak   in the
ceiling
my attention turned   to leisure   beer cans   line the coffee
table
dirt under my nails   soon enough
the kids   will be back in winter coats
the tired cast   still trying   to make
this   home   breaking the hinges   finding a new
route
missing every pothole
& bargain shopper

Lullaby

Repetition of a still frame. A moment repeats itself.
This is the history of our hands opening, this action

of a word unfolding. By "this" I mean precisely this
& the opposite of this. The tension a movement

in opposite directions. Tonight I hold out my hands,
the open palms hold an absence. Rest your head down

on the pillow. Shut your eyes, sweet love. I'll never
tire of wandering these moors. I'll never give up

the search for the proper words. These shattered notes
evenly spaced. This song falling into discord.

A Partial List of Fears

Fear of time travel.
Fear of needles or pointed objects.
Fear of numbers.
Fear of fire.
Fear of asymmetry.
Fear of forgetting.
Fear of poetry.
Fear of Bolsheviks.
Fear of mirrors.
Fear of empty rooms.
Fear of crowded rooms.
Fear of being locked in an enclosed place.
Fear of stairs or of climbing or falling down stairs.
Fear of the color blue.
Fear of waves or wave-like motions.
Fear of dining or dinner conversation.
Fear of dizziness or whirlpools.
Fear of skin lesions.
Fear of objects at the right side of the body.
Fear of objects at the left side of the body.
Fear of having committed an unpardonable sin.
Fear of nosebleeds.
Fear of hearing good news.
Fear of the word fear.
Fear of knees.
Fear of laughter.
Fear of crossing bridges.
Fear of growing old.
Fear of nudity.

II.
Notes & Letters

Yours Truly

The memory of summer unapologetic.
After my mother died, you wrote the nicest letter
& I never wrote you back. The road home
paved with stones & bird skeletons.
This window makes more sense than last.
Emptiness replaced by insight.
Crooked nook, corner stool.
There are many things I will never own.
This dream, for example, is not mine.
I take back everything I told you.

Love Poem to Someone I Do Not Love

You cover yourself
with another blanket
of snow. I wrap myself

inside myself.

You told me not to
go but I went. You told me
to come back but I stayed.

And so I gave you New York,

a pompous gesture
that went unnoticed.
The same as I saw myself

those final months:

a ghost in the landscape,
daily rituals set to autodrive,
& the slow fade

into the background as night

sank into night & you sat
at the bar & flirted
with everyone but me.

As if I could give someone

a city. As if you'd ever want
what I have to offer.

Dear M—

December never seemed so close—this
outstretched hand, a greeting, pulling into.
This bitter pill, a polygraph, caught in my throat.
Tonight: your voice on the radio & how many years
has it been? These bones are old, are brittle & always
breaking. Each day a new face in the mirror,
never quite getting there but always hinting—
I want to be precise: I want to tell you this tendency
is to be discouraged, this leaning & bad posture.
This sketch is merely a moment unfolding, is not
to be taken seriously, nothing like last time
we spoke—two years? three? M, I want to cut
to the chase: I know you understand this failure,
this slow dance, this movement into silence.

I'm not even trying

The ticket lost is long gone.
I've run out of things to sell.
The check bounced.
The phone lost your call
& then I lost your number.
I just put water on to boil.
I became distracted by
the headline: *Five new ways*
to a better body!
The train went express.
I accidentally took one too many
aspirin. I haven't had
my morning cup of coffee.

The Answer

This is all I ask for—to exist. You'd think
I'd want more, you'd think I'd desire

understanding. But I am glad the earth revolves
around the sun how it does. I am glad

the earth's rotation axis is tilted 23.5 degrees
from the sun how it is. You'd think more—

You'd think *never enough, never enough.*
You'd think somewhere else. But no,

these words have nothing more to offer.
You'd think *no, no.* You'd think *naughty girl.*

You'd think *for Christ's sake.*

Travel Notes

7.23.05

My nerves shot from little sleep & too much caffeine.
Drawing birds on napkins. X marks the spot
where the bone broke. A name can be changed
just as easily as it can be forgotten. Setting roses on a coffin
is something I've seen on tv, but also something I've done
in my lifetime. The emptiness fills the house,
seeps into the carpet. Forty-nine years
shuffles through the living room. And the carpet
can be cleaned & replaced but that doesn't really change
anything. I can't explain how I feel except to say
I'm tired. My eyes ache & my thoughts are of my love
in New York. Dear Andy, hello. It is 7:15 p.m.
I opened a beer & my brother is asleep
in the hotel room. Today has felt like two days
& tomorrow it will be forgotten amidst flights & errands.
Last night I dreamt two things I had never dreamt before:
1) I was drunk, knocking over chairs 2) My grandpa.
I was at my grandma's & we were trying to go
to the funeral, but he wouldn't let us leave,
kept wanting to show us things, to delay that moment
just a bit longer. I woke up at 3:48 a.m.
The phone was ringing & it was you drunk on the corner
of Spring & Broadway. Here Detroit is a ghost town.
Nothing to do but jot down these little notes.
Yesterday in London the police shot an innocent man. Today
I buried my grandpa. And tomorrow something else.
My parents are trading the latest news from the gossip rags.
Filling time until morning comes & we each go
our separate ways, returning to separate lives.
The night he died, my grandma slept one hour then
spent the rest of the time just sitting in the living room.

My mom didn't sleep & neither did her sister.
We have never been good sleepers.
Is it normal to feel this old & tired
upon waking to a new day? Or normal not to
recognize the new day, but to have time pass in a blur.
The faces lining up to give their condolences.
A hug & a pat on the back. My brother's flight is at 6:00 a.m.,
mine is at 10:15 a.m. Plan to get to the airport by 9:00
& a cup of coffee or two before that. For now: crime shows
on tv. The forward motion in my chest & stomach.

7.23.05 9:52 p.m.

A margarita later & the world has changed.
I can exercise my trivia skills at any bar. Now, a glass of water
& the family around the tv. Another crime show.
Another escape into Brooklyn. The sky separating into layers,
peeling back from the pavement & tenements. In Detroit
everyone is at the bar, huddled over drinks & glowing television
    screens.
We're waiting on the Tigers. Our lives depend on a baseball
    game.
I can name my favorite Rolling Stones song but can't tell you
how I'll make rent next month. I usually say "Paint It, Black"
but lately have been feeling "Play With Fire."
Andy's on a bus back to Albany & I'm scheduling my morning
wake-up call. Scheduling my shower & time to say goodbye.
A shot of whiskey to warm the body. Every Christmas Eve
was spent in St. Charles, MI. My grandpa would tell stories
about his wilder days, claiming he never would have
gotten married had he been sober. It's a joke & everyone
    laughed.
This weekend I learned my grandpa's birth name was
Francis Antonio Boggio, Jr. & not Frank Anthony,
& that for a brief time he worked, like his father had, in a coal
    mine.

7.24.05

At the airport terminal. Today I woke with no voice.
Last night I tried to explain to my brother that distance
is unnecessary. He said the book was boring, "like reading a
 diary."
On Sunday July 19, 1910, Kafka wrote in his diary:
slept, awoke, slept, awoke, miserable life.
My eyes heavy, no real sleep last night. In the dim light of the
 airport
everything is blurry. Dear Andy, hello. I miss you.
We each have our own separate lives with limited time together.
I wish people didn't hate me but I can't really stop that.
And there are other things to think about anyhow.
The neighborhood is changing & I don't know what I'm doing
with my life aside from working hard for too little money.
Everywhere I move becomes a ghost town. I don't know why
I feel so strongly the need to document this moment, as if I
don't write down, it never happened.
The airport is a ghetto, no place for a home. My nerves shot &
 another cup of coffee.
I can trade sleep for sleepwalking, memories for movies &
 books.
I re-read *The Sonnets* on my flight to Michigan & can't stop
thinking about Berrigan's two hundred graves:
Put away your books! Who shall speak of us
when we are gone? Let them wear scarves
in the once a day snow, crying in the kitchen
of my heart!

Saginaw

Dirty shopping carts
in dirty parking lots.

The future I was promised
enclosed here in this

brown paper bag.
The hustle & flow

of a thousand empty
pockets scraping

against the grey
sky of unemployment.

Who has forgotten
their sons, their daughters?

Forget my dreams:
how things were

going to be different.
Our single state recession

slumps into the new year.
Yesterday's paper

listing today's foreclosures.
My inability to be

what you need me to be.
My only companion,

a 99 cent cup of coffee.
The guarantee of something

bottomless waiting for me.

4.14.06

April snow & no
way to go, no turning
forward, motion lost
flickers across the wind-
shield & is forgotten.
No scene waiting
to be seen, no unforgiving
space, empty drawer
& shutters shut.
Outen the light
on the day, I've no mind
for logistics,
tired with time zones.
Falling backward
a paper cup brushes
the curb. I need
new sleep to wake
new places, new math
to fix my tax return.
April snow & no
one spoke, we just sat
there & let ourselves be
covered. The day
collapses, my eyes
hurt & two cups
of coffee. The window
scrapes & nothing moves.
The shipment sits
in customs.

A Partial List of Fears

Fear of saints or holy things.
Fear of Hegel.
Fear of road travel.
Fear of glass.
Fear of sleep or being hypnotized.
Fear of doctors or going to a doctor.
Fear of voids or empty spaces.
Fear of movement or motion.
Fear of the knee bending backwards.
Fear of cosmic phenomena.
Fear of having to balance.
Fear of words.
Fear of rabies or of becoming insane.
Fear of machines or of robots.
Fear of being bound or tied up.
Fear of memories.
Fear of moths.
Fear of myths, stories or false statements.
Fear of death or of dead things.
Fear of new drugs.
Fear of Nihilism.
Fear of the dark, of night, or of nightfall.
Fear of gaining weight.
Fear of vehicles.
Fear of the figure 8.
Fear of rain or of being rained on.
Fear of snakes.
Fear of being stared at.
Fear of heaven.

ововITIES

III.
Homecoming

Forecast

The sea will flood & flood. Years spent wandering.
Ten years of rain will be followed by ten years of drought.
One year of decadence will be followed by one year of plague.
Our bellies will be full & then they will be empty.
The sun will rise & fall. Day will eclipse into darkness.
We will learn the curve of our spines—the exact arc of our ribs.
The land will turn to ash. Food: ash.
Speech will be whispered. Words: ash in our mouths.
We will no longer trust our neighbors or our families.
We will no longer trust ourselves. Night after night spent in
    solitude.
All questions will go unasked, lost in a landscape of memory.
We will be trapped somewhere between sleeping & waking.
We each will experience our own exile, our own state of waiting.

The Waiting

after Marina Tsvetaeva

The wounded in winter imagine the spring.

The wounded in winter falling
& falling. The wounded in winter set back

each clock.

The wounded in winter keep their dead—they stitch each ghost
to their sleeves.

The wounded in winter

take all the books from the shelves. They whisper *there was
a body, it wanted to live*. The wounded in winter picture
an empty house & burning letters. (Always this burning
for the wounded in winter.)

The wounded in winter count backwards, peel back
the floorboards. Absently they turn
page after page in search of a prayer. The wounded in winter
feel the dirt beneath their nails.

Prayer

for example: a pillar of salt

Drought

Leaves fold in on themselves, words fold in—
color fading at the edges, crisp & shattering

at a touch. Silent bird, sing me a song.
The plants withering, whisper of mistrust.

Who has plucked the voice from your throat?
Who has plucked the rain from the clouds,

the clouds from the sky? Even the sun
is poisonous. All summer going into &

coming out of doors, looking at graphs
& charting numbers, handling dry leaves

of old books. The fingers lose their sense
of touch. The body, no longer hungry.

There is no shade to rest under, just dry air,
absence of wind. Watch the grass burn & burn.

Silent bird, who filled our mouths with sand?
Who said the secret to flying was forgetting to land?

Return

Your words are masks but I speak clearly,
say *it was your hunger that brought you*

here. Week after week you come back
& smile, draw convoluted lines.

Sometimes you keep to yourself, others
you ask for help—as if you cared

what I had to say. I say *you signed up
for this trip*. I say *welcome to the torture*

show. You say you come from the mountains,
you say there are such pretty birds there,

but you don't say it like you mean it.
On a paper plate you draw a face, attach

a string & wear it over your face. You say
you're smiling behind the plate. I say *fine,*

fine, I've had enough. You say *keep quiet
little girl, it will all be over soon*.

January

Days like this are sometimes forgotten, x'd out and shelved with all the rest. There is an absence of birds, although at times their wings beat against my ribs.

Today: a new arrangement of clocks and the branches are bare. I wanted you to know that I believed you when you said this year the spring will be difficult. Snow is falling & won't go away. I just wanted you to know these are the unhappiest of rocking chairs.

This deterioration is common, can be found everywhere, rests in the space between each word, within each word. Mark the way my breath hangs in the air. I just wanted you to know this is a time for heavy blanketing. I wanted you to know this is a specific "I" addressing a specific "you."

What I am trying to say is this distance is troubling. I am trying to say two opposite tendencies are at work here. These thoughts no longer directed towards you, but

the idea of you. I want you to know

the suspension of time, the waiting, the way I've been cut out of my environment and stitched back in.

The Dare

The first room is a ghost—another's hand
pressed into your hand. You, a lost Alice,
tumbling through the dark woods,
your new dress ruined.
In this room, you are your own heroine running
& running & never looking back.

The second room: a coffin. You trace
chalk marks on the wall & with each step
a new face, a new story to be told. You wait.
Sometimes there is food. Sometimes
there is nothing. You remember
chalk on the lapel:
the $x\,x$ for mental defect.

The third room is a fever. You rest
against the door, palms pressed flat
upon the surface. The third room never tells.
The third room burns right through you.

March

Each day's story folded
into squares, little address,
stitching together
this month's narrative.
Today's theme: darkness—

x-ing out the eyes.
This lions roar is ritual—wind
scraping my cheeks.

All month
the ghosts push
themselves inside

the frames hanging on these
walls. They've been counting
each second, digging cemeteries
on the insides of my arms.

And morning: the walk
to the subway notes the return
of birds—their songs breaking open—

Self-Portrait as a Mirror

Hello empty space, hello
constant shifting—

little disaster, little idea
of home always somewhere
out of reach. You might

think edgier. You might think
this is not the way. Perhaps
something else. Something sharper
or shinier, some undefined other.
But no, this is not so.

Do not be deceived—

these words can cut
glass. This emptiness
pushed

inside a frame. This emptiness
is more than you would know:

infinite regression, or a reflection
of a white wall, little bird,
little how-do-you-do.

Sonnet Beginning with Lines by Robert Creeley

I see the flames, etc. But do not care, etc.
I watch the sunset, etc. But do not care, etc.
I'll leave a tip, etc. But skip out on the bill, etc.
I see the spirit, etc. But lost all hope, etc.
There was a crooked man, etc. With a crooked smile, etc.
There was a cause, etc. But it has been lost, etc.
I sing it in the morning, etc. I sing it in the evening, etc.
There established a pattern, etc. But I do not care, etc.
This is something different, etc. This is necessary, etc.
Time passes, etc. But I do not care, etc.
The rain keeps falling, etc. The wind keeps blowing, etc.
I have grown old, etc. I feel it in my bones, etc.
I have grown tired, etc. I sleep all day, etc.
I misremember, etc. But do not care, etc.

The Functioning

To those hands that fix, hurts smoothly
To these hands that repair
To be tended & to become injured
To the father in the end of these hands
To the bowl of fruit carefully picked
To be stretched & to become injured easy
To be tended & to begin again
To those hands when wicked
To those hands when young & unanswerable
To be stuffy & to come to easy injury
To those hands that fix & arrive handsome
To the hands building a new structure
To the hands at the end of the road
To be bent & twisted metal
To be held up for all to see
To these hands folded, secure in rest
To be carefully paced & meticulously planned
To the hands rhythmic
To the smooth hurt in the end of the hands
To these hands beautiful, arriving
To the night of the hands opening
To be lost & to be found in the end of these hands
To those hands that bend smooth hurt
To be hurt smoothly & to arrive
To the ease of these hands
To the ease in the end of these hands

The Dance

Everywhere your stale breath, your tired song.
Smoke collects at the ceiling. Is it fair
to say you made me this way—the crooked smile,
the rotten tooth? Is it fair to say you made me?
The table is dusty & the chairs broken.
I haven't slept in weeks. This isn't how
it is supposed to be—your desire cracks & pops,
makes a left turn. You say you want to make this
home—the broken clock, the rusted nail, the sign
out front that says stop. But you never listen.
Listen for a moment my dear & you will hear
the slight tremble: feel the floor begin to shake.
See the tide turn now. See the rats come running.

Rilke

the death and the life of it the face
of a boy
the person of a boy of it this speaks the death and the life
in the mouth a death and a life in the mouth
read face of a boy the person of the boy
of it this comes from a distance
this comes by far indescribably arrives something
in the mouth the person of the boy of the test
the person
of the boy of the test of it indescribably arrives
a little bit slowly to a mouth the death
speaks it
the death and the life this speaks the death
and the life in the mouth

Perpetual Motion

after Barbara Guest

Under the stone—
trembling. This little dosage.
Instruct a landscape:

a robin dead
on the sidewalk, one wing
sticking up in the air,
as if refusing
to stop. As if it never
needed rest—

to simply say: "No
thank-you, I'm doing quite well
on my own."

Look through
the darkened window:
the poem at midnight.
A row of independent mirrors:
Little ghost, what are you thinking?
What keeps you up?

Carve your face in a tree.
It will always be this way:
the same wrong word.
Instruct a wound.
Instruct a wound to heal.

The Trap

Endearing insistence. Forgetful prey.
This house has burned for 900 nights.

So it goes: tiny comfort, a brief surprise.
The acting out of something sinister.

Wicked little chore, wicked little
here-&-there, burn & burn & burn.

Lonely pioneer. Ignoble officer.
In the box: the framed syntax.

Trace the edges. The rat banking
against the walls. Revile this act.

Sing it twice & it's twice as nice.

Homecoming

All week I've been moving in & out of my body.
Mirror-window. Shadow-self. Trick-or-turn.
The light is gone from the window.
And the curtains, the curtains, unmentionable.

A Partial List of Fears

Fear of spelling mistakes.
Fear of suffering or of disease.
Fear of parasites.
Fear of swallowing, eating or being eaten.
Fear of philosophy.
Fear of daylight or sunshine.
Fear of choking or being smothered.
Fear of beards.
Fear or abnormal dislike of politicians.
Fear of rivers or running water.
Fear of quartets or of being drawn and quartered.
Fear of progress.
Fear of stuttering.
Fear of being tickled by feathers.
Fear of old things or traveling back in time.
Fear of the color red.
Fear of Satan.
Fear of writing in public.
Fear of silence.
Fear of trains, railroads or train travel.
Fear of being evaluated negatively in social situations.
Fear of dependence on others.
Fear of crosses or crucifixes.
Fear of symmetry.
Fear of being buried alive or of cemeteries.
Fear of taking tests.
Fear of the sea.
Fear of one's stepfather.
Fear of picnics.

IV.
A Model Year

A Model Year

The ground shifts but no one notices the spinning.
No one notices the stop light or the time I said no.

Three years time folds into a single instant.
Structures re-build themselves & everyone moves forward.

Always wanting what we can't have, we create tension
one word at a time. Pulling the narrative away until we're lost

& it's lost, left behind in the restaurant or on the subway.
The little bird in the tree re-builds its nest, the cat

watches through the window, wanting. Always wanting
what we can't afford, some leisure time or a casual hello.

Attempting to fill an empty space with anything:
yesterday's news, photographs, a box of buttons &

loose thread. Trying to keep my eyes open after a bad dream.
Don't let me fall again. There's only so much a body can take

but still stupid desire. To attempt a composition, a theory
of migration. Hands gathered in the lap, syntax folding

in the mouth. This testament to a year, a document
of your travels. Something to fill the space.

Something to fill space but still the body waits.
Attention shifts & fills itself with birds in the distance,

a car horn, children throwing rocks in the street.
In the distance, an echo. Thought interrupted by

phone lines. To create structure out of broken pavement,
a cup of coffee or any welcoming thing. Move forward

without hurt. Build your day around re-setting the clocks:
rise & fall & compile a new grocery list.

Sweep the floor on Sundays. It's easy to fall in a dream.
Easy to confuse foolishness for generosity, a bathtub

for a sensory deprivation tank. One day you wake
& everything has changed. Time has erased so much,

taking from you all the people you once loved.
Each movement becomes measured, how

you reach for the change in your pocket.
It's easy for the body to peel after it has been burned.

Easy to push forward & no one will notice
how you reach for change & the leaves turn.

No one will notice when you fall. The ground
shifts & the pavement catches up with you, meets

your chin. And when it happens, the body ages.
Ten years pass but you think instead of youth.

Afternoons spent dirty & riding bikes, tin cans
tied to tree branches. Where once there was a we

there is now an I, an imagined you.
Where once there was a witness to distance,

time folds into an envelope. I am trying to step
outside the body, for the body to push forward, always.

To take a command & go without injury. As if
following orders were as easy as brushing your teeth

or any domestic thing. To make a space for one's self.
The cat asleep in the window. A new set of silverware,

pictures to frame for the walls. Comfort in the most tedious
of things. A way to make the time pass.

A way to make the time pass is as good as any
validation, any idea of happiness, opening

a new book, finding solace in preparing dinner.
Moving to L.A. or Toronto has never been

the answer. The home we built made sense
if only for a brief time. The dream in which I'm falling

& startle myself awake has always been here.
I couldn't watch the images on tv, bodies

hurtling through space. Push inside yourself.
Paint the living room orange.

Buy new curtains to block out the sun. When
you didn't have to go to work, you slept,

filled whole days with sleep. Waking to eat,
smoke a cigarette, have a drink. It's easy to fall

for a dream. Easy to pretend the flowers are blooming
specifically for you, or the walk home a yellow brick road.

Attempt to make sense of wanting, make sense
of the empty seat across the table.

Moving has never been the answer but always
an understandable response to the empty seat

across the table. Threads come loose & the button
needs to be re-sewn. Time to trade sweaters

for short sleeves. The sun on the skin acting
as an agent of love to keep you golden & warm.

To hold you in memory golden & warm.
An afternoon nap in the park. The body continues

to grow, moves forward, guarded.
Memory like loose thread unravels, re-builds,

constructs a new sequence of events.
Remembered faces that were never there, never

a part of this story. Forgive me if I repeat,
I don't know where else to go.

No new words to explain my appearance here today.
No new words for today & waking & sleeping.

I've attempted to re-trace my steps,
looked the last place I was.

Re-trace & re-learn. Return home to the daily
tasks, making pasta in the kitchen the heat

is inescapable. Bare feet flat against wood
floor & it's still two months till August.

The neighborhood is heating up,
more bodies on the street

each day. More voices till the early hours
of the morning. Broken streetlights &

the train passing overhead. Impossible to drink
the glass of water while it's still cold.

When standing in the door of the refrigerator
isn't enough. When the promise of fall &

the return of jackets is not enough. Another year
passes & the body is tired. Falling into a dream,

an escape from monthly bills & worries
of money & debt. When I last dreamed of you,

there was a hole in your side. A fist-sized hole.
I reached for you & reached my hand right through.

The act of reaching for another causes
such misery that it's easy to forget the good.

The memory of New Year's replaced
with the memory of packing boxes.

Every new failure returns to this. The ground shifts
& everything goes on without you, without me.

A car runs a red light & strikes a child on a bike.
The cat licks his claws clean having satisfied

his urge to hunt. The tape rewinds & begins again.
The question of how long things can go on this way

is answered with always, of course.
Always. I know this but still can't stop.

There are no rules for this. Things are easier
when there's a code of behavior. Waiting

for Saturday to pass into Sunday & Sunday
into the work week so one knows what to do

with their time. Language neither the problem
nor the cure, just something to occupy myself with.

No one taught me the softness of the quilt
against my cheek. It was something I could only

learn myself. No one taught me how to deal
with emotion. How to handle restless nights.

& so I lied when I said I didn't know how
I got here: a series of bad mistakes and misjudgments.

A touch of idealism. Hope then disappointment.
Really I've traveled nowhere. Standing in the same place

for three years. Still wearing the same blue jeans,
only now a hole in the knee.

After three years, the skin is a little thicker.
Bruises have come & gone. The body moves

between sickness & health, slips between sheets
each night. There may be new scars, a story for each.

It's easy to pretend nothing exists outside
your four corners, your own little concerns.

Easy to turn off the tv & not read the papers.
It's easier not to make decisions but to just allow

things to happen, hereby escaping any culpability.
Blame it on bad luck & not bad decisions.

A blank page can mean a fresh start or nothing
to say. This line of thought will continue &

I can map its progress, using tacks & colored string.
It's easy to pretend that I'm the only one who feels

this way, or feels anything so acutely. Confusing
one's self for the center of the world, & then

news of a death in the family, a roadside bomb, &
protesters killed by their government shatters everything.

The shattering of everything has become a way
of life. The ground shifts, no one notices.

It's wrong to make either one of us out as criminals.
It's wrong to fill this longing with a haircut

& new shoes. Wrong when we run into each other
on the street to pretend no hurt exists or offer

a casual hello. There are no rules, no guide
to get through the day. Always wanting

what we can't have, the attempts
to make sense of it have failed.

Days progress & add up & the calendar changes.
We pour a new cup of coffee, cover ourselves

with new blankets, separately. The sun shifts
through the window & the cat sleeps, his leg twitches.

It's easy to close my eyes & think of falling. Easy to feel
the body collapse on the bed, the mattress rushing to meet you.

Acknowledgments

The author would like to thank the editors of the publications where some of these poems, sometimes in other versions and under different titles, first appeared: *Cannibal, CARVE, The Canary, Coconut, The Cultural Society, CutBank, The Duplications, H_NGM_N, The Hat, Magazine Cypress, Melancholia's Tremulous Dreadlocks, MiPOesias, No Tell Motel, The Bedside Guide to No Tell Motel: 2nd Floor, Past Simple, Small Town, Tenemos, Unpleasant Event Schedule,* and *Wicked Alice*.

Some of these poems also previously appeared in the chapbooks *Fear of the Knee Bending Backwards* (H_NGM_N B_ _KS) and *Stanzas in Imitations* (New School University).

The poem "Yours Truly" was originally published as a limited-edition broadside by Rope-a-Dope Press.

The author would like to thank everyone who made this book possible, especially Bruce Covey, Dion Mindykowski, Paolo Pedini, and Justin Sirois. Thanks also goes to Jim and Cathy Myers, Gabriella Torres, Matt Heller, Nikki Flaming, Dan Farnum, Jonathan Hirn, Sarah Pierson, Andrew Mister, Shafer Hall, Dustin Williamson, Maggie Nelson, Karl Saffran, Kevin Thurston, Joe Massey, Tony Robinson, David Shapiro, Michael Sikkema, Hazel McClure, Dietmar Krumrey, Nathan Hauke, Joseph Lease, and Donna de la Perriere.

Photo by Dan Farnum

Gina Myers is the author of numerous chapbooks including *Behind the R* (ypolita press), *Stanzas in Imitations* (New School), and *Fear of the Knee Bending Backwards* (H_NGM_N B_ _KS). She writes, teaches, and makes books for Lame House Press in Saginaw, Michigan.

www.ingramcontent.com/pod-product-compliance
Lightning Source LLC
Chambersburg PA
CBHW031211090426
42736CB00009B/875